The Buddha's Gift to the World

Tranquility for a Turbulent Planet

The Buddha's Gift to the World

Tranquility for a Turbulent Planet

Monshu Koshin Ohtani

AMERICAN BUDDHIST STUDY CENTER PRESS

NEW YORK

The Buddha's Gift to the World
Tranquility for a Turbulent Planet

The Twenty-fourth Monshu
Addresses the Twenty-first Century
Volume One

by Monshu Ohtani Koshin

Copyright © 2014, ABSC, New York
American Buddhist Study Center

An adapted translation by W. S. Yokoyama
in collaboration with Mutsumi Wondra,
with the permission of the author. Based in
part on the author's *Yo no naka Annon nare*,
Tokyo: Chuo Koronsha, 2007

Edited by Michael Hayashi in
collaboration with S.B. Yoshikami
Final Edit by Henry Adams

Permission to publish this work was arranged with the
Hongwanji Press, Jodo shinshu Hongwanji-ha, Kyoto, Japan

Library of Congress Cataloging-in-Publication Data
Ohtani, Monshu Koshin,

The Buddha's Gift to the World
Tranquility for a Turbulent Planet

ISBN #978-0-9911360-3-2

First edition 2014

Published and distributed by
American Buddhist Study Center Press,
331 Riverside Drive,
New York, NY 10025, USA

"Monshu" is the title of the head of the Nishi Hongwanji. Literally it means "Master of
the Gate." The present Monshu is a direct descendant of Shinran Shonin, the founder of
Shin Buddhism. In Japanese, an honorific prefix "Go" is added to the word "Monshu"
which shows respect. Therefore, you will sometimes see the Monshu referred to as
"Gomonshu," but the actual word and title is simply "Monshu."

CONTENTS

ACKNOWLEDGEMENT

The Buddha's Gift to the World is the last of a three-book trilogy by Monshu Koshin Ohtani. We are deeply grateful to the Gomonshu and Nishi Hongwanji for granting permission to the American Buddhist Study Center to publish the English translation from the original Japanese *Yononaka an'non nare*. It was an honor to publish *The Buddha's Wish for the World, The Buddha's Call to Awaken* and now *The Buddha's Gift to the World*. Each book gave us a deeper insight into the compassion and wisdom of Monshu Ohtani. As the twenty fourth descendent of Shinran Shonin we can feel his sincere care and compassion he has for all living things. His wisdom and knowledge of Shin Buddhism and the world goes beyond what you can find in text books. He is teaching us what his lineage of Shinran Shonin descendants passed down to him over the past 753 years.

We could not have undertaken these projects without the help and support from so many dedicated Shin Buddhists. My heart felt gratitude, first, goes to Reverend Michio Tokunaga whose vision and wisdom of spreading Gomonshu's works beyond the borders of Japan, so that English speaking people can learn and appreciate the teachings of Shin Buddhism. I am grateful for Michio's friendship and trust which he extended to us in handling these important works. I am so thankful to Ms. Masako Sugimoto for her tirelessly work with Tokunaga Sensei in taking care of all the administrative details that goes into publishing a book, and to The Hongwanji Press who holds the copyright and granted us permission to publish the English translations.

Throughout all three books, the one man that worked so hard on the translations was Reverend Wayne Yokoyama. Thank you so very much for all the countless hours you put into these translations. You are truly our Shin Buddhist unsung hero. For this book I wish to also thank Reverend Mutsumi Wondra for her assistance with the translations. Mutsumi also was a big help in the first book *The Buddha's Wish for the World*.

I wish to thank all the editors; starting with Reverend Michael Hayashi from Kyoto, Japan, Bun Yoshikami from Stanford, CT., and Reverend Henry Adams from San Mateo, CA. Together they enhanced Wayne's and Mutsumi's translation. Reading it now it is almost like hearing the Monshu speaking. For all three books, Rev. Dr. Alfred Bloom was our academic advisor. Thank you, Al, for all the discussions and emails and advice you gave us. Thank you, Arlene Kato for your eye catching book-cover designs, formatting and production on this book along with two other books by the Gomonshu. We are so lucky and fortunate to have you on our team. I wish to thank Dr. Gordon Bermant our ABSC project advisor and the following members of the ABSC Board of Directors: Josephine Seki, Gary Jaskula, and Mark Sullivan for their support and encouragement.

Finally we are forever grateful to Nishi Hongwanji-ha, Honpa Hongwanji Mission of Hawai'i and their temples, Buddhist Churches of America, Bukkyo Dendo Kyokai, and individuals that helped support the publishing and marketing of this book. Thank you for helping us spread Shin Buddhism.

Namu Amida Butsu.

Hoshina Seki
President, American Buddhist Study Center

A Tribute to His Eminence
KOSHIN OHTANI

In Hawai'i, the most fundamental and endearing expression is ALOHA! It is used as a greeting, in welcome as well as farewell and all occasions in the spectrum, and conveys the deepest, fondest, most respectful and sincere feelings from one individual to another. The philosophy of aloha forms the basis of relationships in Hawai'i. Thirty-seven years ago, His Eminence became the Spiritual Leader of the Denomination and we, the Members of the Honpa Hongwanji Mission of Hawai'i greeted his accession with much aloha and anticipation of a new beginning.

In reflection, in His Eminence's (First) Rescript he stated about "Jodo Shinshu and the responsibility of its devotees,"

> *...awakened to the realization that the great Compassion of the Tathagata embraces all men equally and constantly, his is a life of brotherhood and mutual trust in all men. Therefore, he is able to break free from the shell of isolation, egocentricity, and selfishness and become actively concerned with society and its well-being. This also, at once, should be the response of the total Hongwanji organization that will have an open door to the world.*

Then, once again, in 2005, he stated in his message "On the 750th Memorial of Shinran Shonin,"

> *The life of the Nembutsu is walking the path that leads to birth in the Pure Land, illuminated and embraced by Amida*

Tathagata's wisdom and compassion, while maintaining respect and support for other. By realizing through the Tathagata's wisdom, that the source of conflict lies in the self-centeredness of human beings, it is my hope that we will be able to contribute to the building of a world that is free of conflict, where we all can live life to the utmost with joy and contentment.

In order to accomplish this, we should cultivate a broad mind to understand and share the anxieties and feelings of others, create an organization in which we support each other, and transmit the Jodo Shinshu teaching. Likewise, we need to reorganize our institution's framework so that it meets the needs of the times.

In this way, His Eminence has continually encouraged the Hongwanji Sangha to become more involved in shedding light onto and lessening the suffering of samsaric existence. He expressed clearly that Nembutsu Followers out of gratitude for the Unconditional Compassion of Amida Buddha are also concerned about the anxiety that exits in the life of all people, all existence.

Though his term of Leadership comes to a conclusion in June 2014, we, in Hawai'i, will continue to share the Dharma with the aspiration that it will be able to guide all people with its Wisdom and Compassion. At this time, on behalf of the Members and Supporters of the Honpa Hongwanji Mission of Hawai'i, I would like to express my fondest and sincerest ALOHA infused with profound gratitude to His Eminence Koshin Ohtani for his great insight and leadership. In awareness, joy and gratitude, Namo Amida Butsu/Entrusting in the Buddha of Imeasurable Life and Infinite Light

In gassho/anjali,
Eric Matsumoto,
Bishop of Honpa Hongwanji Mission of Hawai'i

INTRODUCTION

It is both a pleasure and an honor to be asked to offer an introduction to the English translation of our Monshu, Koshin Ohtani's *The Buddha's Gift to the World*. I believe it to be a perfect companion to previous translations of *The Buddha's Wish for the World* and *The Buddha's Call to Awaken*. As a Jodo Shinshu minister, seeking to offer the Nembutsu teaching to people born in the West, I have found these translations incredibly helpful and I trust that this volume will be, also.

The Gomonshu begins with a firm declaration of the Jodo Shinshu position on the Buddha's teaching. We are an "Other Power" religion. As such, we can never adopt the position of telling anyone else how to approach, or interpret the Buddha's teaching, as they seek to manifest their connection to it in their daily lives. We can only foster and encourage each person's relationship with Amida Buddha, as we earnestly seek to deepen our own.

Having said this though, the Gomonshu also recognizes that, simply because of his birth into time and space, being the leader of the largest religious denomination in Japan, he has been allowed to encounter his life from a vantage point that most of us do not have. His feelings of responsibility and duty towards his position, as well as the support he has been blessed to receive, give him a unique perspective that, if not shared, would be a wasted opportunity. Therefore, the Gomonshu presents his insights and suggestions as "proposals". That is, these are not edicts given from on high; they are thoughts we may avail ourselves of as we nurture and support our connection to Amida Buddha and to each other.

The part I find most beneficial to my own efforts to relay Jodo Shinshu Buddhism in North America is the fact that the Gomonshu personally lived through Japan's recent adoption of Western economic and social values after their economic bubble burst in the 1990's. The combination of being a highly intelligent and insightful person as well as having the responsibility of leading a very faith-centered religion during this time led the Gomonshu to form opinions from which we all can benefit. He is fully con scious of the positive effects this change has produced while, at the same time, being keenly aware of some of the positive values Japan may have lost track of as it rushed to adapt to a rapidly failing economy.

As is common with all of us, we are born into a context and we adopt our society's value system without thinking, or even realizing that there may be other ways to view things. The advantage of listening to people like the Gomonshu, who have recently adopted the North American world view, is that those of us born into it can gain a bit of perspective. Inherent biases and flaws, that we may possess and which we may simply gloss over in believing we are "right" in having them, might be revealed to us. Whether we choose to act on these insights, or not, that is for us to decide. I am just glad that the Gomonshu has taken the time to share his experience. I have always found him to be a source of pointed and, yet, gentle encouragement and I am sure that you will also find this to be true.

I am grateful to the American Buddhist Study Center for facilitating this worthy project. Thank you for letting me be a part of it.

Namo Amida Butsu
Tatsuya Aoki
Bishop of the Jodo Shinshu Buddhist Temples of Canada

OUTLINE OF LECTURES

The Gomonshu begins with an outline on Buddhism and society. This outline was originally handed out to college students at Ritsumeikan University in Kyoto, Japan, who attended his Buddhist lecture. Following the Outline is the actual lecture he gave at the university.

I. Modern Society and Buddhism

What religion means to the Japanese

A. The confusion of terms. 1. There is no new word in Japanese to sum up and express religion as a whole. 2. The modern Japanese word for "religion" (*shukyo*) is of recent derivation and imbued with Christianity or Christian-centered concepts of religion.

B. Religiosity in the broadest sense is like a vitamin supplement. 1. Psychological activities as they bear on human existence beyond the practical. 2. Spirituality, is regarded by many as having nothing to do with religion. 3. Funerals without religious affiliations, memorial stones, memorial events, healing.

C. Religiosity in the general sense is like herbal medicine. 1. On paper it emphasizes its principles but they are vague and its permissible range is broad. 2. There are people who talk about religion and those who don't. 3. The shrine, shrine Shinto, sect Shinto. 4. The established religious orders of Buddhism in Japan (to be lost in transmigration versus awakening enlightenment).

D. Religiosity in the narrow sense is like modern medicine

whose efficacy and side-effects have been clearly de-monstrated. 1. The principles they emphasize are clear, they have an institutional structure. 2. There is a resis-tance to importing new ideas and new organization, somewhat less open to society or the world at large. 3. Christianity, Islam (Lord as Creator), new religions (Humans as Gods).

II. Buddhism in Japan Today

The present situation of traditional Buddhism in Japan: the good and the bad.

A. Founder's teaching (individual practice and salvation) and activities of the sangha (our role in society).

B. Funeral Buddhism

C. Religious beliefs being used to propagate war

III. The Suffering Society

IV. A Proposal

A proposal to address societal problems

A. Let us dispense with dualistic thinking: right and wrong are tentative, not absolute.

B. Let us redefine what we think of when we speak of progress and development: rethink our sense of values.

C. Let us plumb the inner depths of what it means to be an individual. 1. Let us realize our interconnectedness with Life (interdependence, brotherhood). 2. Let us awaken to our self-centeredness. 3. Let us awaken to the preciousness of Life (the intangible quality of living).

V. Taking the Edge Off the Demands of Life

VI. Promoting Mutual Understanding Among Religions

I. Modern Society and Religion

Welcome students!

As you know from the previous introduction, my name is Koshin Ohtani. I am the twenty-fourth Monshu in the Jodo Shinshu Hongwanji-ha lineage.

Having only a single hour to address you, I fear that I will not be able to cover everything as I would like to today. Having said that, I am very pleased to have what is for me a rare opportunity to speak to a college-age audience.

I would like to start with the fundamental and defining tenet of Shin Buddhism, or Jodo Shinshu, as it is commonly known. Doctrinally speaking, we Jodo Shinshu Buddhists emphasize "faith alone". That is to say, we believe we are saved by surrendering ourselves and leaving the problem of our salvation entirely up to Amida Buddha.

It is most commonly thought that Buddhism requires us to perform religious practices—that we, through our own efforts, have to perform certain actions in order to reach enlightenment; and that these actions include such things as upholding Buddhist precepts as well as other such religious practices. When we examine the extent of what is required to gain enlightenment through such a method, we find that most of us, if we are being entirely honest, come to the conclusion that this method of attainment is impossible. In our school of Shin Buddhism, we do not make such demands on our followers. We simply ask that they leave the problem of their salvation solely up to the power of the

1

Buddha's Name, *Namo Amida Butsu*. This is the defining feature of Shin Buddhism.

Since upholding the practice of celibacy is not emphasized, it has been the tradition in Shin Buddhism for our priests both men and women to marry. This tradition was established in Shin Buddhism by our founder, Shinran Shonin (1173–1263), who himself was an ordained priest and was openly married. I am not saying whether it is good or bad for Buddhist priests to get married. All I am saying is that it is our tradition for our priests to get married. This characteristic is what set us apart from the other Buddhist sanghas existing during the time of our founder.

I trust all of you have received the outline for my talk (*Appendix*). Please do not worry. I do not intend to cover it in its entirety. The outline merely presents some themes in which I have a personal interest. I present them to you as food for thought.

Let us begin by the word "religion". The word "religion" occupies a somewhat dubious place in Japan today. The mere mention of it is enough to make people shy away. Apparently, there are quite a number of people who react in this way. Therefore, it is thus a pleasant surprise for me to find so many of you enrolled in this present series---that, in participating today, you are trying to come to terms with religion in spite of its lack of popular appeal.

The first thing we should note regarding the word "religion" is that only since the Meiji period (1868-1912) has the word *shukyo* (religion) come into common usage in Japan. *Shukyo* itself is a translation of the Western word "religion". In the West, when you say the word "religion," it is Christianity that comes to mind as the primary example of a religion. With the influx of Western culture into Japan after the Meiji Restoration of 1868, Christianity and the word "religion" entered the Japanese lexicon as meaning the same thing.

While a segment of the population may have welcomed its

arrival, to the Japanese mind, Christianity was a foreign religion. The vast majority of the Japanese did not understand its situation and felt that something threatening had arrived at their doorstep. There was a time when our Buddhist forebears even tried to drive Christianity out. At the popular level, religion in the form of Christianity was received as an unwelcome guest. It is perhaps due in part to this historical baggage that the word "religion" today leaves most Japanese feeling somewhat less than enthusiastic.

When my son entered university, he went to a real estate agent in Tokyo to find a place to live. The agent showed him what was being offered. As he looked through his options, he came across one listing that interested him. However, the owner had written a stipulation: "religious people need not apply". He asked the agent about the listing and told him that he was from a family connected to a temple. The agent told him that temple people were not a problem. He seemed to be saying that, to the owner of the apartment, a temple is not considered part of a "religion". He told my son that they had previously lent the same apartment out to someone from a temple family. It seems, from this example, that what Japanese ordinarily mean by "religion" is used to mean everything outside the traditional temples and shrines of Japan. This example reveals the ambivalence in the minds of the Japanese with regard to the word "religion".

The range of religion from broad to narrow

The outline that you have divides religion into three categories: religion in (1) the broadest sense, in (2) the general sense, and in (3) the narrow sense. Putting aside the question of which one is better, we arrive at these three categories when classifying religion as covering a range from the broad to the narrow.

In the broadest spectrum, what is religious today would come to include things that ordinarily we would not call religious—as I allude to in the items on my list. When we narrow the gauge a bit, the shrines and the established Buddhist temples come into focus. Narrow it even further and we come to religious establishments that make themselves the center of attention.

These religious establishments are strictly organized, hold to a clear ideological orientation, and have definite criteria defining whether or not one is a member of such an institution (or institutions). But, at the same time, ordinary persons outside these organizations may see such religious establishments as foreign-derived religions, or they may see them as being so new that they cannot warm up to them. As a result, they feel quite uncomfortable with them. This is often the case with such religious organizations.

Thus, when we speak of "religion", it depends on what category we are applying when we use the word; otherwise, we run the risk of being misunderstood. As an aid to understanding, I have compared them to being like supplements—that is, herbal medicine and modern medication. These are merely analogies that hint at meanings and are not to be taken literally.

The narrowest gauge of religion can be compared to the medication prescribed by Western medicine. Take an anticancer medicine, for example. While we cannot make an across the board statement regarding all anticancer drugs, we can at least say that while a certain drug may be effective for cancer, it most often destroys healthy cells at the same time. Such side effects are far from small, and in some cases they are so great that they considerably weaken the body.

This analogy includes religions that have a clear ideological orientation. Such religious teachings may have a powerful effect that can completely change the life of a person. At the same time, just one misstep and its other unintended side effects take over. The side effects can wreak havoc on a person's life.

Let me add that I believe our Shin Buddhist congregation tends to occupy the middle ground. Within our congregation, there are all kinds of people: from those espousing radical views to others who merely go through the motions when worshipping before the altar. Because of the egalitarian nature of our teachings, our congregation is naturally a mixed group united by a shared intention to rely on Amida Buddha.

Next, I would next like to turn our thoughts to what religion is. I will leave its final definition to the experts, but as for me, religion is a framework that gives us an ability to recognize spiritual activity. It is found particularly in human beings and forms the basis of our understanding of existence and life. In short, it is that part that makes us human.

Our conventional existence as human beings is a highly unstable affair. It only takes a small change in our outward situation to reduce us to a jittery, nervous and uncertain state. This is not just a matter having to do with our current historical time but is evident in every generation, in every culture, and in every historical period. I would like to suggest that the main role of religion is to address this problem and to guide people as to how to bring a settled, calm feeling into their lives.

All living creatures not only humans have a very strong desire to survive. It would be foolish to think that we can ever go beyond this basic instinct no matter how strong our spiritual realizations and convictions are. But if a person simply exists, that is not enough to resolve the problem described above. There is still something more that we all want. In timeworn terms, what people want is to never grow old, to live to a ripe old age. They want everyone in their family to be safe. They want money, status, and fame. They want all the things they can well do without, yet can never have. This alone causes them a great deal of suffering and their feeling of restlessness grows. It is in suggesting ways to deal with this situation is where the importance of religion comes into focus.

II. The Buddhism Of Japan

Let us consider the present situation of Buddhism in Japan. When seen through the eyes of priests like myself and although though we cannot give a detailed account of the other schools, we know that each individual Buddhist denomination has its own distinct nature. And so when young people come to visit our temple, some of whom are from religion-affiliated schools, I have to talk to them about Buddhism in a more general sense. I always remind them that the Buddhism they see with the eyes is only its outward shell; that from this point on they must learn more about its inner core.

This is like a *manju* bean bun. We see only the white outer shell, and while that is important, the white *anko* bean filling it contains is that about which we want to learn more. This does not mean that the inside part alone is important. Just the *anko* bean filling does not a bean bun make, since that alone would not taste like a *manju*. The outer shell made of different ingredients with its particular taste is also necessary to experience the real *manju* bean bun.

In the same way, as far as religious activity goes, one aspect that is most readily apparent to us is the funeral and memorial services that have earned temples the inglorious name of "funeral Buddhism". As important as these ceremonies are, there is one more important aspect to this, and that is the question of what deeper meaning this ceremony is trying to reveal. This, however, is not a simple matter to get across to the people taking part in the service. This is where we as priests find it hard going and this is where we tend to get impatient with ourselves.

With this as a starting point, let us inquire into the present situation of the Buddhist congregations in Japan today. In Japanese Buddhism, among those who are regarded as its patriarchs or founders, we find the names of such ancient figures as Kobo Daishi and Dengyo Daishi. Then in the Kamakura period, there is the founder of our congregation, Shinran Shonin and his teacher Honen Shonin. There are also other famous names from the time such as Dogen Zenji and Eisai Zenji and Nichiren Shonin. Each of them was highly individualistic, each had high-minded philosophies, and each hammered out his own doctrinal positions and implemented them in lives of religious practice. They are revered as the symbols of the congregations that they established.

When we as priests think of the reality of our lives and the way that an actual temple is run today, and when we place it alongside the way of our founders thought and lived, we would find that these two approaches do not quite mesh. One person put it well: he described the congregation as a religious teaching without practical temple activities to apply to, and as a religious institution without a real religious doctrine to uphold.

As college students you can draw a parallel from your own experience in education, that is, there is a great disparity between the abstract ideas you hear discussed in the classroom and the actual political and economic activities taking place in the real world. It is where these two sides manage to come to terms with each other that the fruits of such activity are produced. In the case of the temple and the Buddhist congregation, that gap or disparity is an important thing to recognize and of which to become aware.

Historically, in the insular world of the past, especially during the Edo period (1603-1867), society was fixed; parent and child and their subsequent offspring were expected to keep up the family business and to live in the same place. This meant that people felt a very close relationship with their local temple. However, this is not the case in the present day and, in the temples currently, there is a lingering sense that we should be doing more to fulfill our societal roles.

The term "funeral Buddhism" is often used in a negative sense to criticize Buddhism. Today, funeral Buddhism finds itself in a critical situation. The funeral and the memorial service, when seen in the light of the Buddhist teaching, has its own redeeming value, hence are not without meaning. It is through the fact that people die that a person is forced to seriously think about what life means. This is true for the person facing death as well as the healthy people around them. We should not put the ramifications of this important learning opportunity out of our minds.

The current problem is that, most often, the funeral is all that the temple does. The temple makes no effort when it addresses something unrelated to the funeral.

Another problem is that the way the funeral is now conducted is unsuitable for the lifestyle of the present age. The funeral has to be conceived anew from a new perspective. There are all kinds of problems that present themselves from a structural and organizational standpoint, but the importance of our experiencing death firsthand is something that cannot be emphasized enough.

In the olden days, large numbers of infants and small children would die due to a variety of causes such as malnourishment and other causes. With the advent of medical science, there are few mothers and fathers who currently have experienced the sorrow of losing a child. Again, at a prior time when there were few hospitals, the sick, in most cases, were looked after at home and usually died in the home setting. Today, this role has been taken over by the hospital, and we have little opportunity to come into an immediate, personal contact with death. For that reason, the younger generation has little opportunity to face the deeper concerns to which religious thought applies.

As a result it is not until later in life, when a person can see their end approaching, that they are suddenly struck by the serious nature of the problem. At last we become fully conscious to what religion has been trying to tell us all along—a message as real as today. Taking the opportunity to consider this problem and holding an interest in it while still a college student is, I think, a wonderful and invaluable experience.

The Outline has a line in it that reads "In Praise of War"—I used this phrase deliberately to shock and arouse your interest. When we look back on the history of Buddhism, traditionally and fundamentally, there is existent a foundation of peace and of not taking up arms that goes back to the founder Sakyamuni. In spite of this, there are countless cases of nations being dragged into participating in war due to the pressures of world politics. In this regard there are many ways for us to evaluate such developments. Also, there is wide debate today concerning such areas as war, human rights, discrimination, and so on. It is important for Buddhism to play a vigorous role in voicing its opposition to war and taking a stand in order to exert an influence.

III. The Suffering Society

"The suffering society," the next item in our Outline, directly refers to war. War is the biggest headache of all for those of us who claim to be religious. Religion, from the outset, has peace as its objective. Could it be that, as some people suggest, religion itself is the cause of struggle? At this point a number of interpretations are possible. When we look at any real case of war, it contains numerous elements that play off and influence each other.

We must keep in mind that when we talk about religion, this does not refer simply to faith in the abstract. There are religions where religion is identified with the entire daily lives of its followers. Islam is an example of this. In Islam, it is not possible to draw a dividing line between the religion and the cultural life and customs of those lands.

We might say the same about the Japanese way of thinking which is inspired by Shinto and which is thoroughly identified with Japanese life. When a religion thoroughly permeates the life of a people, whenever a war breaks out, it is extremely difficult to say whether it is a religious war or not.

My impression is that it is virtually impossible for religion itself to lead to a great confrontation or quarrel, much less to a war. It is, rather, a struggle for economic power or a dispute over territorial rights, or it is about today's problem of poverty; that is, it is about cases where people are struggling to survive that leads directly to war. Naturally, the religions that those people hold will tend to accentuate the more righteous aspects of their teaching in an attempt to unite their people. When these people mobilize for war, it would appear to be a religious war. However, viewed from another angle, there is a strong argument that the war most often results from a territorial dispute or an economic struggle.

Also, war gives rise to the problem of discrimination against the religion of another person. In recent times, in Europe and America, especially among those in countries where Christianity forms the mainstream religion, the drift of opinion is decidedly set against Islam, and the chances of reaching a mutual understanding and acceptance are virtually nil. In a work called *Orientalism* (1978; Japanese trans., 1993) its author Edward Said (1935-2003) criticizes Westerners for forging an image of Islam that works solely to their advantage and allows them to propagate a very negative view of Islam.

What we as Japanese should do when we wish and seek to learn about other countries is to take note of the source of that information. I would like to especially ask the newspaper and mass media people to look at Islam through the eyes of the Japanese people, to look at Africa through Japanese eyes, and to be extremely circumspect when releasing news straight from European and American news agencies. Even today Europe and America look down on other countries. I believe that the Japanese people can look at other countries through different eyes than those in Europe and America.

Further, so as to avoid the onset of war, it is important that we treat with respect the things that our counterparts respect the most. When we encounter people from a different culture, it is natural that we come away with impressions like, "I can't understand what their religion or philosophy is all about," or "their culture is strange", or "those people are so inscrutable", but that does not mean we can say something bad about them by concluding "That's why they are no good", or "their culture adds up to nothing". Unless we are careful to treat them with respect, we will make the mistake of injuring the very thing our counterparts treasure the most, and in so doing we will only add fuel to the flames.

Here's an example from preschool: two little children wind up fighting because one of them got mad because one said something bad about the other's mother, and soon they are having a go at one another. For little children, the one thing they won't take is someone badmouthing their mothers. That gets them fighting mad. The thing that makes this a parable of sorts is that this is not limited to children. If we show a respectful attitude toward the things that are most cherished by our counterparts, and though not going so far as to be gushing with empty praise for them, nor by becoming a devotee of their faith, I believe that this is one way to prevent war from spreading.

With regard to the question of religious cults, there are times when I am not sure what to think. It is indeed a perplexing problem. But at least I would say that we should think of the leaders and the followers as being in two separate categories. Those who follow cult leaders and live by obeying their authority without question are living an extremely dangerous lifestyle. When critical inquiry is not allowed, our perspectives can become skewed very quickly.

As I said at the outset, our Jodo Shinshu congregation is established on the principle that faith is all; that we must leave everything up to Amida Tathagata. While it is hard to place a premium on doubt from this perspective, the problem with religious cults is that they need to allow this element of doubt, or at least questioning. The fact that there is currently nowhere in modern society where such followers can turn, and also that there is even a mechanism in society that gives such people no choice but to turn to religious cults—these are problems that need to be addressed.

IV. A Proposal

Among the items of the Proposal given in the Outline, I would first like to consider the role of dualistic thinking. When we think on something and, at the same time if we consider it in terms of good or bad, or plus or minus, it then becomes easier to deal with. The present computer age is a binary age, where there are simply the choices of either one or zero. However, when we have to deal with world problems or the problems that people face, and if we use this simplistic approach, it is possible for important points to fall between the cracks.

Consider Buddhism's basic philosophy which is expressed in terms of the concept of *Engi*, Skt. *Pratityasamutpada*, or Interdependent Co-origination where everything comes into existence as a whole, all at one time, and is a result of the interrelatedness of all things. (Let us note in passing that the popular Japanese phrase *"Engi ga ii"* or, *"Engi ga warui"* "What a lucky coincidence!" or vice versa "What an unlucky coincidence!" has the word *engi* in it, but its meaning is entirely different.) To depend on the Other rather than oneself for one's existence means that everything exists in a living network of indirect and direct causes. There is no individual existence, nothing perpetuates itself forever. This is the concept of Interdependent Co-origination that is the cornerstone of Buddhist thought.

With this as a starting point, let us look once again at today's theme. When we apply a simple dualism to things, we end up deciding that "this is good and that is bad." Is this not dangerous ground on which to tread? When it comes to thinking in terms of good and bad, we should especially recognize that, usually, it is "we" who are the "good" and those who are against "us" are the "bad". If we look at the present American foreign policy, it would seem to be built on this kind of simplistic dualism. Will this not lead to the further spread of war? Just as the world we live in is made up of friends good and bad, it is the nature of the world to be made up of many different kinds of components.

There is a related topic in Jodo Shinshu thought: it is the teaching that the wicked are the object of the Buddha's salvation. The superficial conclusion this leads to is that, if one has to be wicked in order to receive the Buddha's compassion, then I will not be saved unless I commit some terrible crime. In such a scenario, serious-minded students like us are left out in the cold for we have no intention to ever commit a sinful or criminal act.

With regard to this idea of "that the wicked are the object of the Buddha's salvation," regardless of whether you have committed good or bad acts, as long as you surrender yourself and leave the problem of your salvation to Amida Buddha, you will be saved — that is the gist of our way of thinking. However wicked a person might be, the problem turns on whether or not that person surrenders his ego and leaves the problem of his salvation to Amida Buddha.

But the other thing to consider is the following: is committing a terrible crime the only criteria used in determining what a wicked person is? When we set up the problem on the basis of a simplistic duality of good versus evil, we come to the point where we must ask ourselves whether we really belong on the good side. If we explore this further, we arrive at a religiously important issue: the more we become aware of this question, the more we feel what Buddhism teaches penetrates to the very core of our being.

Furthermore, in Christianity and in Islam, the notion of a contract is an important element. In today's economic world, the word "contract" is also an important component. This notion is said to derive from the contract between God and man. Since it is a contract, if one does not uphold the contract, this "breach of contract" means one must receive some kind of punishment. When we consider whether the wicked will be redeemed within the framework of such thinking, a person who does bad things has violated their contract. Hence, they should not be saved, or so goes the rationale of this line of thinking.

In Buddhism by and large, however, such notions as contract and promise do not exist. The goal Buddhism sets up for itself is to go to the rescue of those who have lost their way. And the person who is lost, once they realize they are wandering and lost, naturally returns to the correct path—this is the basic thinking here. Thus, it is not a person who is mistaken that must be punished. A person who is deep in the state of bewilderment must be quickly pulled out of it. More than one who is in the shallows, it is the one who is drowning in the deeps that must be rescued first—this is the thinking that applies. It is not a question of which of these is the finest of individuals, but rather, it is a question of who is it that is in immediate need of rescue.

To give another example of dualistic thinking, there are a lot of people suffering from hay fever these days, and I am one of them. But the cause of hay fever is varied. One cause is air pollution, but another is that our natural resistance to hay fever has diminished. This is due to the absence of the action of intestinal parasites in people. This is what one researcher reports.

In Japan today, such intestinal parasites are virtually non-existent, but in my generation, I remember there were many students in elementary school who had tapeworms. At school quite a few students had to take medicine to rid themselves of these worms. Apparently, the tapeworms in the intestines produced some kind of substance that worked to suppress other allergic reactions.

What that researcher tells us is that, in today's drive for cleanliness in Japan, we have gotten rid of all the dirty things, so that everything from the socks up, wherever bacteria may lurk (and such microbes are everywhere) must be disinfected and sterilized. The upstart is that, if we examine the human body, we realize that we are alive because of the living network of microorganisms of all kinds that come to our aid.

We might have some reservations to thinking that tapeworms actually help us humans. However, the point is, unless we have the full regalia of various intestinal microorganisms, the human body cannot live. To simply divide good from bad, to say all germs, bacteria, and parasites are bad, and to say that, if we get rid of them then we won't get sick, is simply not true.

What at first glance may seem dangerous to us turns out to be a team of germs and other microorganisms that support the life of the human body—that, thus, we live by mutually supporting one another. I was impressed by this finding. Man does not live only by what he can see alone — this is what this perspective allows us to consider further.

From here, the line of argument may be somewhat rough to follow, so I hope you will take a cue from it to develop thoughts of your own.

The problem of brain death and organ transplant is one of the great topics of modern Japan. The general trend has been in favor of promoting the concept of brain death in order to allow us to harvest transplantable organs. In regard to this and in contrast to the number of religions that have come forth with position statements, the Buddhist standpoint is seemingly unclear. I have even heard criticism over the fact that Buddhists have yet to say anything substantial on the issue. Of course there is no clear-cut Buddhist standpoint that we can take. It would not be surprising to find opinion varies from one person to the next even in the same doctrinal stream.

With regard to organ transplant, what I am about to say is not a variant opinion. Consider the situation purely in the case of brain death. First of all, the word "brain death" occupies a highly dubious position. Usually when we lose the use of a hand or a leg, we would not say "my hand is dead", or "my foot is dead". Previously, the expression we would have used was that the organ in question had stopped functioning. At some point this expression was changed to "the brain is dead". And it is here that questions arise as to this line of thought.

The main problem is the idea that, if the brain is not working, it must be dead. In order to do an organ transplant, fresh organs have to be obtained from a living donor. Once a body dies it is useless. And so, the medical profession interprets the fact that when the brain has died, the person also has died. This draws a distinction between the brain and the body. The idea that the brain is everything, presents a form of dualistic thinking separating the brain from the body.

To use a metaphor of organization in society, the brain is much like an army. Although I have never seen one, the army has a command headquarters that issue orders that are relayed to the front line. Thus, if the headquarters are captured, the entire army falls apart. Though less familiar to me, in a corporate structure, the front office management acts as a brain to set up policy and the employees act as its body to carry this policy out.

The problem that I have with this kind of model is whether it is right to force a multi-faceted human being into this mold. That is, I am unwilling to leave everything to the doctors and medical profession to be the sole decision makers with regard to the problem of the human life experience of birth and death. I would rather that people with a background in humanities and law also be allowed to enter the discussion.

The interpretation that, if a brain no longer works, and that this fact is taken to mean that the human person is dead should not be a problem to be decided solely by the medical profession. It is an extremely important topic and those in the humanities with philosophical and religious backgrounds need to be involved. Thus, even though you may not be medical students, I would instead urge you to turn your thoughts to it and study and investigate it further, rather than saying this topic does not pertain to my specific subject, so I do not have to consider it.

With regard to progress and development, it is true that the times change. The Japan of today is quite different from that of old. From my school days, our society has pursued this image and goal of progress and development. It is undeniable that science and technology have undergone great progress and development, but I would contend that the human person has evinced no such progress. Things such as politics and society undergo change, but there are aspects of it that show progress as well as those that simply do not.

If someone were to say that religion is old-fashioned or that Buddhism is old-fashioned, I would agree that, in form and expression, they tend to be old-fashioned. But the issues that religions attempt to interpret have not changed from ancient times to the present. I believe it is the mission of Buddhism to assert itself and bring those issues to the forefront of current thought.

Some things show no progress, such as our short and limited life, as an example, or how the human being is an animal that always seeks for what is best for itself. These basic features show no signs of progress. A person starts from zero, makes an effort to live and experiences different things that help them grow, — there is that facet. Then the next generation comes along and again a person starts from zero and grows some years reaching a limit around the century mark. The human race as a whole, however, exhibits no growth, and it is in this aspect that religion takes a firm stand to address the issue in question.

Finally, the preciousness of human life is a major issue for religion. To mete it out logically, however, is extremely difficult. Some years ago, someone posed the question, "So, why is it wrong to take human life?" to which a number of well-known figures were hard pressed to answer adequately. Even if we were to say, "It is because life is precious," it is hard to proceed beyond that. But rather than set forth a logical explanation, I think it is far more important to arrive at an understanding through our life as we have physically experienced it.

First, with regard to the modern issue of how society has become so harsh that it treats people as mere commodities, we need to look at the problem from a slightly different angle, ask what we must do to treat people as human beings, and how to respect them as vessels of life. There is one detail from everyday life that we may tend to overlook: the Japanese word *Itadakimasu*, or "I thankfully receive this from you," which we say before a meal. In our congregation, we say this special word before a meal as an important religious ritual. It expresses our thanks to other life forms for the life we receive from them. But when too much emphasis is placed on it being a religious rite, it has its drawbacks; such as when public schools begin to feel reluctant to use it and will even want to eliminate it by issuing a statement that it is unsuitable to the classroom, as has sometimes happened.

It is a key contradiction of human life that man must partake of the life of other living beings in order to live, no matter what word, or concept we choose to express our recognition of this fact. The word *Itadakimasu* bears within in it all kinds of feelings, such as, "I'm sorry to do this", and "Thank you very much". And so for us who cannot live without taking the life of other living things, the least we should do is pause for a moment to express our feelings of contrition for this less than noble deed that we must do.

Or it could be that you were raised lovingly by your parents and those around you, and as a result you feel that your own life is a precious one. From that experience, you want to treat as precious the lives of those around you as well as the lives of the coming generation. Your understanding together of how precious life is deepens through such real and tangible experiences, even though you may not consider them to be experiences that are particularly religious.

Well, that is all the time that we have for today. As this is the end of my portion of the series, I would like to thank you very much for your consistent attendance and for listening to my talk to the very end. *Arigato gozaimashita.*

V. Taking the Edge Off
the Demands Of Life

When we think of the state of the Japanese mind today, one thing that I am deeply taken aback by is how little value people attach to life. In recent years, the number of people who take their own lives has gone past thirty thousand annually. Many of the cases are middle-aged and elderly people, who are the living heart of our families and of society. Some people explain this trend as being caused by the economic straits these people are in; many after having lost their jobs due to the restructuring of the economy. At another level though, this points to the problem that human beings are crumbling from within. That is my sense of the matter: that people are suffering from a breakdown inside.

Thinking back, I did not have the sense that people were reaching their limit during the bubble crisis of the 90s. Looking at the people in the midst of the economic crisis from a religious perspective, I thought the Japanese people were actually holding up rather well. After all, it is not necessarily a bad thing for people to experience an economic letdown, or so I thought.

But after the number of suicides started to climb and soon doubled above the annual number of deaths occurring from traffic accidents, I had to admit we had a terrible problem on our hands. At the temples we noticed more and more people, who had lost family members due to suicide, coming in for counseling. People were at a loss how to deal with this outpouring of grief. These strident voices began to be heard with increasing frequency.

The newspapers these days carry so many cases of terrible,

violent incidents that after a few months it is hard to keep track of them all. Most of the recent ones make no sense. They happened because a person was having a quarrel with someone else, or they were displeased about something someone said, and so they committed a violent act. It is not as though they had no more money left and were forced to steal. Most cannot explain why they would intentionally injure someone else. This is the perplexing aspect of many of these cases.

The Buddha said, "Remember that you are much like them. Do not kill others and do not cause others to kill" (*Dhammapada* 130). If your wish is the wish to live, then in order to guarantee the safety of your life, you have to be willing to guarantee the safety of others. When the Buddhist teachings set down five precepts that all people must follow, the very first one was that one shall not take a life. This is considered a fundamental edict for the continuance of a decent human life.

With fewer and fewer people living with their grandparents these days, the opportunity for us to witness the death of someone close firsthand has dropped to almost zero. Because we have fewer chances to experience the intense pain of separation from those whom we love, it has come to the point where we even have to explain to people why it is wrong to kill other people. It is a shocking age in which we now live.

People taking their own lives, people taking the lives of others — either way the person who does so does not have a sense of themselves as being truly alive. When they lack this sense of being vitally alive, they regard the life they have as being of no particular importance. They see the lives of others also as being of no particular importance. In this way, people who do not think twice about taking their lives are similar to those who will go out and injure others without a thought. Our present society is one where there is no solution in sight for this serious problem and it is growing worse and worse each day.

Now as we look at this serious problem facing family and society, we must ask ourselves what we must do. When asked about a solution from a Buddhist standpoint, I would have to say that I am sorry but there is no quick and easy answer to this problem. Indeed we must look this serious problem straight in the eye.

That is the starting point for the process. Up to now Japan has gone ahead and solved its problems in a haphazard manner. Mostly, we simply patch things over, hoping that while we are distracting ourselves with other thoughts, the problem will solve itself. This might have passed as a solution in a different age.

These days the word healing is in vogue. It is true that Buddhism has an element of healing to it. However, it is in no way correct to say that healing is the goal of Buddhism. That completely misses the mark.

For example, let us take the situation of a businessman who is reassigned to another section where he does not feel any eagerness to work. If that is indeed the way he feels about his situation, he will end up thinking his job situation is hopeless. If you look at the problem in the light of Buddhism, our thinking this-and-that about our job situation is a secondary problem. It is quite understandable that, in any new situation, one might feel reluctant at first to go forward. What Buddhism aims for is a loftier goal. It is what I call "the Life process of liberation".

This might not have any immediate bearing on the problem of how it is we are to make a living, but we need to turn our eye to the basic question of why it is we are living in the first place. Even if we have our relative strengths and weaknesses, man is originally born with nothing. There are those rare individuals who are so gifted as to be called geniuses, but, for the most part, most people are like us—ordinary mortals. Certainly, there might be a tad of difference in our abilities, but most of us just have to plod on and do the best with what we have. If we are lucky we will encounter the right circumstances that allow the full range of our abilities to come into play.

When I hear people say things like, "I have to find someplace to better put my talents to use" or "Oh no, unless I can keep on working here, I will be ruined", I detect in such words a fixed way of thinking from which they stubbornly refuse to budge. If this small bump in the road is really enough to stop them from living, they will find that life has some mighty harsh surprises in store for them. Eventually, they will find that illness will force them to take time off work or that this attitude may cause their own performance at work to drop.

There will come a time for every person, whoever they may be, to become acquainted with sickness and old age. The preparations for that outcome should be set in motion whatever age we may be. No matter who you are, at some point in time, some sort of disease will force you to experience for yourself a world you never knew existed. It will make you realize there are a lot of things you did not know about the world. It just might occur to you then that Life has a lot more waiting in store for you.

If we do not let ourselves be hemmed in by the hard shell of our ego, if we follow the flow of change in whatever direction conditions lead us, if we remain flexible and accept the changes as they come—than this outlook is a much better way to lead a more positive life by receiving what Life has to offer us.

When you put all your hopes into one fixed goal, such as sending your child to a famous private school, all it takes is just one false step and then all is lost. But, it could well be that a different way awaits you—a place where you will feel more inspired to live if you were to follow such a path. There are many true stories of people who came to live more active lives due to finding an unexpected opportunity that took them from the line of work they initially sought to pursue. These are people who are good at receiving whatever Life has in store for them. Of course I cannot say that I have any direct experience in the world of competitive business where the hardships there are impossible for me to imagine.

I was fifteen when I received *tokudo*, the first ordination in our School of Buddhism. That was in 1960. In the olden days in Japan, it was the custom for children to follow in the footsteps of their parents. It was less common for someone to make the individual choice to start out in an entirely different line of work. That was the way it was with the Hongwanji lineage for hundreds of years. At that age, I of course knew I still had to grow up a bit more, but I followed in my father's footsteps and proceeded down the Buddha Way. Since then, I have been blessed by having good people around me, who have let me creatively pursue my work and, whenever I could, I tried to be of use in my role, even in some small way.

It was not until my first year of high school that I moved to Tokyo, where I lodged at the house of a temple family related to the Hongwanji. It was completely different in my father's case. He had to move to Tokyo from elementary school where he stayed with the family of a college professor who raised him. After college he enrolled for a stint in the military. It was not until the age of twenty-five that he got married and settled down in Kyoto. During this time, he lived entirely separately from his parents. In my case, it was not until high school that I left home and so it was relatively late. In the case of my own son, he was raised at home until he completed high school and it was not until college that he left for Tokyo.

The reason my father sent me off to Tokyo was so that I could learn there things that I could not learn at Ryukoku University in Kyoto. In short, I could experience what I needed to know to become a priest. That was his plan for me. At Tokyo University, I enrolled in an Indian philosophy course where I could study Buddhist teachings. There were not many students enrolled and almost all my classmates in the program were from temple families like myself. If there was someone from a different denomination, I was fascinated to meet them for they practically amounted to being someone from another culture.

With the advent of the modern age, people wondered how they ought to understand the ancient teachings of Buddhism. This doubt grew even stronger for those of us born in the postwar era. Up to then, people read the Buddhist sutras in Chinese translation that was then translated into Japanese. That was our way of studying and understanding Buddhism.

It is to the credit of Professor Nakamura Hajime of Tokyo University, who encouraged us to deal directly with the Indian Sanskrit Buddhist texts and to read them in modern Japanese. When we read the words of Sakyamuni Buddha (Siddartha Gautama) in modern language, we found that they contained teachings that made sense even now. I was very moved by the discovery.

The Buddha's words, "For hatred does not cease by hatred at any time. Hatred ceases by love. This is an ancient truth" (*Dhammapada* 5), is a sharp admonition that could well be leveled at the present age. After the war, the San Francisco Peace Treaty Convention was held. Although every country affected was seeking reparations from Japan, the Ceylonese minister J. R. Jayawardene gave a speech explaining why Ceylon would not be seeking any reparation from Japan and quoted this famous passage. It was this Buddhist spirit that came to Japan's aid in the postwar period.

If we can set aside hatred, a world of peace would prevail. These plain and simple words contain an eternal truth. It is a jewel of wisdom of the Buddhist teachings with which I would like all people in the modern age to be more widely acquainted.

Reflecting on the recent war in Iraq brings to forefront the limitlessness of human greed. Though various factors can be cited as the cause of this conflict, what it boils down to is the struggle over oil as an energy resource and this factor of greed is the biggest cause of that war. I cannot help but feel that simple human greed has been blown out of all proportion in this case.

Some people will say that religion is always involved when a war flares up. That might be true in a sense. In the case of Islam, more than in the case of Buddhism or Christianity, religion is tightly interwoven into the daily life of its people.

If there is any struggle with the Islamists, it is certain to involve their religious viewpoints. At the same time, I think there is no such thing as a struggle between friends who claim to have no religion. Religion has a role to play whenever troubles arise. This is simply a consequence of living. Thus, it is not unexpected that religion should show its face when a heated struggle takes place.

However, the question is whether religion moves to incite war or whether it moves to quell it. Here the responsibility of those who are deeply involved in the religion becomes a point of focus. For instance, a terrorist act of blowing oneself up is only possible because it has a religious background to support it.

When we look back on the history of Shin Buddhism, while it teaches that we should put out the flames of greed and anger, its past also records the struggle of the Shin Buddhist-inspired peasant uprisings of the Ikko ikki. As for modern day Buddhism during times of war, it is sad to say that our teaching stood there powerless to do anything to quench the flames.

Now I would like to touch on a few points of the Shin Buddhist teaching. Earlier we touched on the five precepts of Buddhism. They are: not to take life, not to steal, not to commit adultery, not to lie, not to drink. In Shin Buddhism there are no such restrictions, that is, Shinran Shonin, founder of Shin Buddhism, was not one who set down regulations about what people should or should not do. In his own case, he had to lead the strict life of a Tendai monastic on Mount Hiei for twenty years from age nine to twenty-nine. Even so, he was not able to purge himself of his human passions. That is, he experienced for himself the impossibility of liberating oneself by one's own powers.

It is only natural for man to have human passions. If you try to snuff them out by force they will only come snaking out in some other form. We have to seek and walk the Middle Path, which is neither to give in to our all-too-human desires nor to seek to purge ourselves of them. The key point here is that it is better for one to understand the predicament of having desires.

The other day, I saw a political cartoon in the newspaper that showed two men on a sinking ship fighting over the first class suite. This is not to say we should deny the desire to seek status per se. There are those who want to attain status and there are those who want to see other people achieve status. After all it takes a certain kind of person to become a politician. They have to have the desire to attain status otherwise they will not strive for that goal.

People may understand the dangers of the desire for power, fame, and success, but all the same they may be swept away by it. When their goal is in sight, they think to change the world yet again for the better. They cling to a goal of ever greater meaning, and, thereby, give in to their desires even more.

There are many people who are familiar with Shinran Shonin in association with the saying that the wicked person is the goal of Amida Buddha's salvation. This statement is found in the *Tannisho*, a thirteenth century book compiling some of the sayings of Shinran Shonin. There is a famous passage in the book that goes: "If the good man is granted his wish to be born in the Pure

Land, how much more so is this true of the wicked!"

The Shin Buddhist teaching casts light on the fact that all people in the world are wicked. They are led around by their desires, they trample on the weak in order to live, they take the lives of plants and animals in violation of the precept of taking life. It is in this sense that all people are wicked. It does not mean that we should work at being wicked or that the wicked are considered to be privileged.

When we consider the matter a little more deeply, however, it seems to me that the confusion comes in when we try to judge people on the basis of good and evil. There are not two kinds of people in the world, one good and the other evil. While there may be cases where we might speak of "the wicked" in a relative sense, a greater problem arises when we fall into the trap of self-pride and assume that I am all good, I am the good guy, I am in the right, — such thinking leads to hate and anger toward others. It could easily lend itself to becoming the seeds of war. We must thus realize that there is a dangerous side to the word justice.

Indeed, there are those who are prone to break the law, that are dangerous to society and, as such, they are beyond society's salvation. In the classroom they are a cause for concern to parents and teacher both. Such children pose a problem and we would rather they be brought into line. Or, we might think of them as someone who has fallen overboard and is drowning. From this perspective, the first consideration would be to go to their rescue. It is in this sense, that those we consider wicked are the objects of salvation in Shin Buddhism.

Another Shin Buddhist teaching is expressed by the words *Tariki hongan*; most often translated as the Other-Power of the Original Vow. In modern Japanese, this is often used in a sense divorced from its original Buddhist meaning. A recent popular work on Other Power has done much to correct this misperception and give the phrase a positive image. Commonly though, it is used to mean "making no effort on our part and depending on the efforts of others to solve our problems," that is, to take a *laissez faire* attitude. This is an misunderstanding and is caused by a focus on our conventional understanding the words "other" and "power."

Shinran Shonin says that Other Power is the power of the Nyorai's Original Vow; that is, it is the working of Amida Buddha. Whenever I think of this phrase, *Tariki hongan*, the Other-Power Original Vow, to my mind it is the Original Vow part of it that presents a problem for the modern mind—not the part of the "other power". After all, whose original vow are we talking about, anyway? It is the vow or wish made by Amida Buddha for our world, but it is working from beyond the realm of our human desires. So often we, who are encased in those very desires, do not notice it working. It is a vast universal wish that goes beyond the limited wishes of our human world.

A Buddha is one who has turned the wishes he has made into reality. Among the forty-eight vows made by Amida Buddha, there is one that says that he will surely save all living beings. Thus, when Shinran Shonin says that "other power" is the power of the Nyorai's Original Vow, it means that our salvation is realized through the power of Amida Buddha's Original Vow and we are born in the Pure Land. This is what Shinran Shonin is revealing to us by using the words "Other-Power Original Vow."

As a result, whenever we try to realize our own wishes whether by our own power or by powers other than our own, what it involves is completely unrelated to the Buddhist teaching. The basis of Shin Buddhism lies in whether we are able to understand and accept the wish of universal salvation that Amida Buddha has for us that goes beyond the limits of our human power to realize.

Shinran Shonin started off with the version of the Pure Land teaching that taught that, if we successfully do the religious practices to attain enlightenment, then we will be born in the Pure Land in the life hereafter. However, not everyone is born in such fortunate circumstances where one is able to engage in the religious practices of a renunciant, one who leaves all of his societal and familial responsibilities behind to live the life of a monk. Shinran Shonin sought a path of salvation in the present world for such people such. The same is true for us today in being bound to our lives. Shinran Shonin found a path for us. But unless people in the midst of their ordinary lives understand and accept Amida Buddha's Original Vow, Shin Buddhism will go nowhere.

What is necessary then is for modern people to understand the principles of the doctrine. There are plenty of opportunities for this to happen. Someone once gave a sermon where they pointed out that you cannot see the wind but you can see it rustling the leaves of a tree or hear the tinkling of a wind chime. Based on the existence of these observable things, we know there is a wind. Likewise, we know of the power of Amida Buddha's Other Power from its presence in the lives of people it has transformed. We can also know of it from the written documents that they have left behind after they died.

The sun rises in the morning and sets in the evening. This is a phenomenon we are all familiar with and it imparts in us a religious feeling. But these days, the chance to experience this sentiment in the midst of our busy modern lives has become rare. In recent times, there are many children who have not seen the sun set. In Shin Buddhism, the sun setting in the west is an important image of the Pure Land in the western direction. It is difficult to have people experience this feeling of associating the Pure Land as being west of us where the sun sets, if such an image or connection has not been fostered in their lives.

As for things I am able to realize in my day to day life, by my act of saying "Namo amida butsu," I leave all of that up to Amida Buddha. The Nenbutsu I say during the service is said with a level of lightness as if I were paying a call on Amida. Namo at one time might have meant "I believe in you." It derives from the same root as the greeting *Namaste*, or "Hello, how are you!" used in India and Nepal. For those of you who resist saying the Nenbutsu, I would recommend that you set some time aside to say it, perhaps, five or ten minutes a day. I think you will find that it will sharpen your senses. Just a word of caution though: if you imagine that the Nenbutsu is your own practice and you do it with all your might, I think you will hardly find any change taking place.

My father died in June, 2002 at age of ninety. As I watched him slowly growing old, there were many thoughts that crossed my mind regarding the process of growing old and dying. I recalled the words of the *Tannisho*, "As reluctant as we may be to leave this world behind, when the conditions for remaining in this Saha world run out and our life force is spent and it is time to meet our end, it is at that point we are brought round to that Land" (Shinran Shonin as quoted in *Tannisho* 9).

My mother passed away before my father. Toward the end of her life, she was hospitalized many times. Whether her room had a view of the mountains and greenery or whether there were only concrete buildings visible from her window, this all made a big difference on how she felt on any given day. In our busy lives, we do not even glance at the grass growing by the roadside. However, when you are in a hospital room, your eye finds the greenery in the distance and you find yourself thinking, "Ah, there is still life going on all around me." These are things you notice for the first time once you fall ill.

With my father, the nurses would often comment on how wonderful his smile was. Buddhism talks about the seven priceless gifts we can offer others for free. This includes the ability to regard others kindly, to look at others with a gentle expression, and to be cheerful. I like to think that this was his way of repaying the kindnesses of the people around him.

My classmate from elementary school days was told that he had only six months to live when he was diagnosed with lung cancer at age fifty-six. He actually lived for two more years, but he had no desire to buy new clothes, since he did not want to waste money that he could leave to his family. In the midst of his suffering, however, he was able to compose a book of poems. In these poems, he takes a deep look at life and expresses his thanks to his family and friends, as well as to the living world around him: the trees, grasses, and flowers.

One day you suddenly learn that the life remaining to you is limited and you can no longer live shut away in your shell. And you find yourself transformed into someone who thinks solely of repaying the kindness shown to you in the limited time left. After experiencing the loss of my close friend, I find myself thinking of how to round out the years remaining to me.

A person is bound to grow weak and age. This is nothing to be ashamed about. To accept the years gracefully as they pile on is one of our last rites in life. The older we get, the less able we are able to take care of ourselves. I had the impression that toward the end, it took my parents all their effort just to get through each day. Their example taught us, their children, what a great effort it took just to live. At the very end when they passed away the feeling that naturally rose up in my heart was *Gokuro sama*: thank you, mother, thank you father, for everything you did for us while alive.

We are now being overwhelmed by the so-called health boom. It would seem that health has virtually replaced religion on the list of things for which to strive. While masses of people are drawn to foods and different health techniques that are supposed to be good for you, behind this search there lurks their strong fears over growing old, getting sick, and dying.

Even healthy people cannot get entirely rid of their apprehension about getting ill. It is thoughtful of them to call on someone in the hospital. However, when they think to themselves, "I'm so lucky I'm healthy, I'm in much better condition than that guy," this is a sign of their arrogance that, in this way, they look down on other people. Both the person who still has their health and the person who has lost it are both necessary for this world.

Lately, people talk about their funerals openly. To me, the funeral itself ought to be left to those who survive us. I sometimes think it is going too far for one to become too involved in planning one's own funeral. It is as if we were extending our ego beyond our death. While I am alive, I would like to face the reality of death and give it some serious thought.

As I said before, the present age is an extremely difficult one in which to live. In olden days there was a natural pattern where both living and dying were understood to be integral aspects of life. With the advent of science, our lifetime has been extended. But when coupled with the problem of the looming low birthrate, the prospects of growing old are not always happy ones. Sometimes we hear people say things like, "it is a good time to make a baby". It would seem that these people think that life is a treat that they deserve and that they are the masters of life and can "make" life at their convenience.

Life is something that we have received from beyond the limits of human power. It is in the chain of events making up life in which life has been built up on this earth with each individual being added one by one the last 3,500,000,000 years. It will not do to look on life lightly, by making it into something we feel we deserve.

As we pass the baton of life to the next generation, it is important for the older generation to firmly impress upon the younger generation that we are alive only because the conditions supporting our life are in place. When we live in this way, each day brings new discoveries. This is the secret to living through the worst situations together, even though we are ordinary people loaded down with human passions of every kind.

VI. The Buddhist Contribution to Peace Through Promoting Mutual Understanding Among World Religions

Buddhism and Peace

I am convinced that the Buddhist teachings contain many valuable hints as to how to bring about world peace by reducing the differences between world religions. For instance, there is a saying attributed to Sakyamuni Buddha, the founder of Buddhism: "For hatred does not cease by hatred at any time. Hatred ceases by love. This is an ancient truth" (*Dhammapada* 5). I believe that these words have a universal message that speaks to people everywhere. Of course it is no easy matter to dispense with hatred, but it would be far more productive to think of how to relinquish hate, rather than apply our minds on how to retaliate against others.

A recent newspaper article quoted an elementary school student as saying, "First there was an act of terrorism and retaliation against it. And then there was another act and again retaliation. At this rate what is going to happen to this world of ours?" The Buddha said, "Remember that you are much like them. Do not kill others and do not cause others to kill" (*Dhammapada* 130).

He also said, "Blissful is solitude for one who's content, who has heard the Dhamma, who sees. Blissful is non-affliction with regard for the world, restraint for living beings. Blissful is dispassion with regard for the world, the overcoming of sensuality.

But the subduing of the conceit "I am" — that is truly the ultimate bliss." (*Muccalinda Sutta, Udana* 10, Thanissaro Bhikkhu trans.) That is, he realized that it was the lack of wisdom on the part of living beings that was the root of their suffering. He saw that suffering was caused by the unrestrained influence of their raw human passions.

Nakamura Hajime, a professor of Indian philosophy, once wrote that "resorting to violent means in order to realize peace was what the Buddha abhorred most." However, if we ask whether the Buddha's teachings have been effectively handed down by the monastic community and whether they have had an impact on society at large, I think we would have to admit that they have not. Likewise, while Mahayana Buddhism espoused the noble ideal of the salvation of others above the goal of achieving enlightenment for oneself, this ideal has not inspired us to grow beyond our self-centeredness to any large extent. In recent years, however, we have seen the emergence of an engaged Buddhist movement. This is evident especially in Southeast Asia where Buddhism has become involved with applying its professed ideals to societal problems. This is a movement to which we should pay close attention.

A concept highly expressive of the Buddhist worldview is *pratitya samutpada*, or interdependent co-origination, J. *engi*. Basically, the concept states that every seemingly separate "thing" in the world arises out of a mutually shared set of conditions and as such there is nothing that lasts forever. For example, dualities such as justice and injustice or friend and foe would seem real enough, but they come into existence only because the conditions that support them are there. In fact, they have no reality in and of themselves. We recklessly jump to conclusions when we resort to violence to eradicate them. It would be better if we took things into perspective and sought to bring about real change by addressing the underlying conditions that gave rise to them one by one.

All life on earth as it interacts with physical conditions is mutually supportive of one another, and if only one species were to dominate all the others, it would end up driving itself out of existence. It is only through our mutual relationship with water and air that life becomes possible for us as human beings, as well as for flora and fauna. Even the terrible events and individual sufferings that occur on this earth are all linked together in an intricate network of mutual relationships, and though we may not be able to eradicate them completely, at least we must strive to positively affect them when we are able. This is because I am a part of the whole.

Let us next consider the Buddhist concept of compassion. In Japan today, people tend to talk more in terms of love and affection while the word "compassion" has gone out of vogue. Here, while most people would think that love is the opposite of hate, I would like to point out the significance of compassion as standing in contrast to indifference. The kanji *jihi* for compassion is thought to have derived etymologically from the Sanskrit *metta* and *karuna* meaning "friendship or parental love" and "pity or empathy," respectively, with the connotation of removing a person's pain and imparting them with joy. It is for this reason that the kanji *jihi* has been translated as compassion, rather than love.

The Buddha is recorded to have said, "As a mother would risk her life to protect her child, her only child, even so should one cultivate a limitless heart with regard to all beings" (*Karaniya Metta Sutta, Suttanipata*, Thanissaro Bhikkhu, trans.). Also, "To all, a friend; to all, a comrade; for all beings, sympathetic. And I develop a mind of good will, delighting in non-malevolence — always" (*Theragatha* 648, Thanissaro Bhikkhu, trans.).

Since Buddhism basically points to a way of leaving behind our delusions and to opening up to enlightenment, those who have yet to attain enlightenment are the object of salvation as well as the object of pity or compassion. Never should they be considered the object of punishment. *Pratitya samutpada* provides the firmament for compassion, where there is no dividing line separating the savior from the saved. They stand on the common ground where your sorrow is my sorrow and your joy is my joy. When we turn our thoughts to the problems of the Middle East, before passing judgment on matters in terms of good-bad, justice-injustice, benefit-harm, or profit-loss, should we not first feel their sadness and suffering? It would be merely relative of us to think dualistically in terms of good and evil or right and wrong like the rest of the world.

Shin Buddhism is the teaching established by Shinran Shonin. It is, in part, the founding spirit of our university and it informs my life as well. By opening up the teaching of religion to everyone it characteristically sets out to accept all the bad karma of human beings. Through leaving the matter of our salvation entirely up to Amida Buddha we go to the Pure Land where we attain enlightenment. Here we see the mode of existence of Amida Buddha as wholly intent on going to the rescue of all living things, regardless of whether they are good or bad. From this we know that Amida Buddha has vowed to save all living beings equally, his activity transcending all distinctions of race or nationalities.

The limits to our wisdom and abilities being what they are, we keep repeating the same mistakes over and over, and yet we have to keep on trying to live while going to one another's mutual aid. As we are too inured by our all-too-human passions, I do not believe we can ever realize a perfect peace. Nor should we think it possible to side with our limited viewpoints and seek a one-sided peace where one power tries to hold sway over the rest. With regard to the sentiment that war would disappear if everyone in the world were to become a Buddhist, or that war would disappear if everyone one became a Shin Buddhist, I would not deny the thought in principle, but realistically speaking this is impossible. It would be the height of arrogance to compel others to become Buddhists or to think that there is no other path to peace other than Buddhism. And most assuredly this stance would invite deserved criticism from the followers of other world religions.

Promoting Mutual Understanding Among Religions

In recent years, I have noticed that each religion tends to use the word religion in its own special way. This leads to mis-understandings among them. Subtle nuances come into play when a Westerner uses the word religion and the Japanese use the word *shukyo*. One similarity we share with the West is the separation of politics and religion. One difference turns on whether or not our particular religion is an orthodox feature of our society.

While the separation of politics and religion is taken for granted in the West, this is because Westerners think of religion as standing on a par with state and politics. It is only through a long historical process that politics and religion have arrived at this arrangement with Christianity as the representative religion in the West. In Japan, however, the situation is somewhat different. There are many people who regard religious congregations such as Christianity as creeds of foreign origin, hence not on a par with state and politics. Although they would not hesitate to call them religions, all the same they think that such religions should remain separate from politics.

Incidentally, while the researchers at our national universities undertake academic studies in religion in what they believe to be objective and methodological ways, a recent study by a scholar named Nakata Ko criticizes the fact that the concept of religion employed in these studies often assumes that the essence of religion is individual and internal, and that, as such, they are in fact deeply endowed with a particularly Protestant interpretation of religion (*Shukyo kenkyu* 341, Sept. 2004). He criticizes the fact that, while studies of religion are ideally objective, they can be criticized for assuming the separation of religion and politics as being orthodox. As for Shin Buddhism in particular, its primary experience, which is that of receiving the entrusting mind of *shinjin*, is an event which takes place internally. As such, it would also tend to affirm the separation of religion and politics.

In the nineteenth century, a sense of crisis spread throughout Japan when the Western powers began to make inroads into Asia. After the Meiji Restoration (1868), heated debates took place over the question of whether Christian missionaries should be allowed into the country. We also witnessed the birth of several new religions around this time. The Japanese word "*shukyo*"; used to translate the word "religion", can be traced back to the beginning of the Meiji period (1868). In light of this fact, the newly coined word *shukyo* bore with it the nuance of being a foreign religion, beginning with Christianity, as well as the nuance of being a new religion associated with strong individual religious beliefs. In the process of producing a state Shinto that was compatible with the freedom of religion, Shinto was said not to be a religion, but a set of societal rituals and ethics.

While religion was assumed to be separate from politics even in Japan, at the same time it was considered to be incompatible with Japanese tradition and was seen to run against the grain of orthodox thought. When you ask the average Japanese person what their religious beliefs are, many of them will reply that they do not align themselves with any specific religion. From a religious studies perspective, however, many of these same people have a religious mind in the broadest sense and may even participate in various religious rituals spontaneously. That is because they do not consider the rituals of everyday life to be religious. Since this is the situation that we have in Japan, it is only to be expected that misunderstandings will arise when we try to talk about what religion means with anyone other than a scholar of religious studies.

There are generally a lot of skewed perceptions and mis-understandings about Islam in Japan. Even I myself am guilty of a few. I understand that Edward Said's masterpiece *Orientalism* did much to change the perception of Islam in the West.

Now let me ask: How should the Japanese perceive Islam? After all from the Western perspective, Japan is also considered the Orient. In spite of this, the Japanese wholly swallowed the Western perception of Islam. They never tried to let their gaze dwell on Islam and form their own opinions. The problem is closely tied up with the "leave Asia, enter Europe" sentiment of the Meiji period, as well as the complex and opaque problem of Yasukuni Shrine. On this occasion, I hope this symposium will provide an opportunity for people to deepen their understanding of Islam.

In Islam, there is characteristically no distinction drawn between religion and everyday life. They form a perfect unit. Islamic regulations cover every corner of daily life making it difficult to separate the actions of Muslim believers from their religious beliefs. When a conflict arises in a Muslim country, it is surely considered to be of a religious nature. When violence is employed, it is surely considered to be of a religious nature. We should also note that, when non-violent means are used to help others, this too should surely be considered to be of a religious nature. To the Japanese mind, since Islam is involved not only in doing good but also in doing things which are not good, the average Japanese would say that Islam is a religion that is dangerous and frightening, but such a critique does not lead to any productive discussion on Islam. It is essential that we start the discussion with the religiosity of Islam first and place that foremost in our minds, as we think about a way to peacefully engage it.

The Shinto of Japan marks a great departure from Islam in the sense that it does not give a clear account of its doctrine. On the other hand, they share many similarities in their ability to unify the communal body. Like Islam the Shintoist philosophy fills every corner of daily life. Since it does not distinguish itself from worldly affairs neither does it acknowledge the separation of politics from religion. In this respect Shinto shares a similarity with Islam. And, while the rituals that Shinto conducts at its shrines are clearly observable events, less accessible to the eye are the vast majority of its other practices and customs performed in daily life which are linked to the Shinto sense of values.

Since the separation of politics and religion does not apply to Islam, the Western observer as well as the Japanese find Islam difficult to comprehend and are inclined to interpret it negatively, but from one perspective, I think it possible to say that Islam shares many points in common with Shinto.

When people in Japan gather to discuss what religion's role should be whenever a conflict or war occurs, or what it should be in promoting peace, they express different opinions that are opposed to one another. For instance, some will say that religion is the cause of conflict, while others will say that the cause of the conflict lies elsewhere, — that social and political activists are merely taking advantage of religion to achieve their ends. No doubt both opinions contain a grain of truth, but rather than generalize, we need to look at who each speaker is individually.

As mentioned above, many people in Japan will say they have no religious affiliations. When such people say that religion is the cause of conflict, then they have a perfect rationalization for shirking their responsibility for causing the conflict. On the other side, there are the naysayers like myself who are involved in religion, who will try to absolve themselves of responsibility by saying that religion is being abused by the activists. In the territories ruled by Christianity and Islam, the tendency is not to place blame on their own religion as the cause of conflict, but rather to pass the blame to the religion of their opponents.

What convinced me to take this stance was the observation that in any religion there are always two types of people: there will be those who will make their own religion absolute and will refuse to recognize other religions, and there will be those who will see the value of their own religion and yet acknowledge the existence of the other religions.

The opportunities for religions to come in contact with one another have now increased due to the rise in global interactions. When such encounters occur, there are two ways the other religion can be viewed. On the one hand, one can take the offensive and deny the validity of the other religion by saying it is wrong. Those who take this approach, hide their heads in their shells when they say that the only true religion is their own. On the other hand, there is the relativistic approach, where one says that all religions have an element of truth to them and so whatever religion it may be, as long as it is a religion, then it is good.

The latter, the relativistic view, is what generally tends to prevail in Japan. When one adopts this view, though, one is apt to lose one's own genuine viewpoint. This is the ever-present danger of viewing matters from a third person perspective. When relativism goes too far, a reaction to this is that the fundamentalists start to dominate the scene. This is what we are seeing in Japan today.

To my way of thinking, it is important for each of us to hold our own religious traditions dear, all the while seeking some way to coexist with the ideas and values of other religious traditions. To achieve this we must strive to understand our counterparts in other religions and never treat their symbols or rituals lightly or disrespectfully. This is most important. It is of course no easy matter to attain a profound understanding of a religion that is not our own. For those who profess to have no religion at all, it must be doubly difficult to understand any religion at all.

To make fun of a religion just because you find it hard to understand, however, does not do one bit of good and is only harmful in every way. When children start to fight they get so excited that they start insulting everyone including their parents. When they sully the atmosphere of the household in this way, it only creates bad feelings all around. As a result, things get out of hand and nothing is really resolved. It could be that no one is physically injured, but this does not mean it did not leave some kind of scar inside.

In Europe this winter (2005), a set of cartoons published in a newspaper as satire blew up into a serious controversy because they touched on Islam. It is indefensible to make fun of the religious symbols of another tradition saying that it is our right to do so in the name of so-called freedom of the press. Such irresponsible actions only stir up conflict in society.

Satire is meant to loosen up an uptight society. At times satire is also used to voice the despair and unhappiness of the oppressed. In this case, the cartoons did not represent the pleas of the weak to the strong. If it were meant as a social critique, it would have been better if they had used other images, not religious ones. My conclusion is that this was clearly a case of religious abuse.

When our communal body is endangered, it is necessary for it to receive the support of religion, and religion seems to fully fulfill this role. At the same time, it is necessary to exercise discretion in order not to overdo it. We need leaders who have a clear idea of what they are doing. We must be careful not to take the "we are right, they are wrong" attitude. While we must take pride in our own religious tradition, at the same time, we must learn to understand and accept another's religious tradition. This is the greatest challenge for religion today.

SOURCES

The Buddha's Gift to the World. Originally published as *Yo no naka, Annon nare: Gendai shakai to Bukkyo*, Tokyo: Chuo Koronsha, 2007, of which this is a freely adapted version, with the author's express permission.

V. Taking the Edge Off the Demands of Life.

Originally published as "Let's prime the senses for a few minutes each day: How to take the edge off the demands of life expertly" 一日五分、五感を磨き澄ませよう、人生の厳しい現実を上手に受け止めるために *Bungei shunju*, March, 2004.

VI. Buddhism's Contribution to Promoting Mutual Understanding Among World Religions.

Originally presented at a Ryukoku University seminar with the theme of "The International Context of Conflicts in the Middle East and Asian Approaches to Conflict Resolution" at the First International Symposium of the Afrasian Center for Peace and Development Studies in March, 2006. Original title: "Heiwa: Sho-shukyo no sogo rikai to Bukkyo no koken" 平和: 諸宗教の相互理解と仏教の貢献. We have referred to the abridged English translation presented at the event. It was very helpful when it came time to make our own version that includes the complete text of the original paper.

The Gomonshu's Books in Our Series

The Buddha's Wish for The World, hardbound and paperback, 2009

The Buddha's Call to Awaken, 2012, 2014,

   and e-book 2014